Apples and Pears

WORKBOOK D

American English
Edition

Hilary Burkard
& Tom Burkard

First published 2016, Hilary Burkard

ISBN: 978-1-905174-30-0

PUBLISHED BY HILARY BURKARD

DISTRIBUTED BY
SOUND FOUNDATIONS
www.soundfoundations.co.uk
mckenzie@soundfoundations.co.uk

Apples and Pears

Review :

Date: _____

Part 1.

1. _____   2. _____

3. _____   4. _____

5. _____   6. _____

7. _____   8. _____

1. _____   2. _____

3. _____   4. _____

5. _____   6. _____

7. _____   8. _____

Part 2.

1. _____

_____

2. _____

_____

Part 3.

1.   fun + y = _____ + est   = _____

2.   en + joy = _____ + able = _____

3.   scare + y = _____ + er   = _____

4.   spray + ed = _____

5.   angry + er = _____

6.   de + lay = _____ + ing   = _____

7.   boss + y = _____ + est   = _____

Apples and Pears

Part 3. Continued:

1. _____   2. _____

3. _____   4. _____

5. _____   6. _____

7. _____

Part 4.

1.   state + ion = _____

2.   ob + ject + ion + s = _____

3.   ac + cept + ed = _____

4.   re + ceive + er = _____

5.   de + vise + ion = _____

6.   photo + graph = _____

1. _____   2. _____

3. _____   4. _____

5. _____   6. _____

Part 5.

1. _____

_____

2. _____

_____

Apples and Pears

Date: _____

Part 1.

1.   im + pose + ing = _____

2.   re + vise + ion = _____

3.   tele + scope = _____

1. _____   2. _____

3. _____

Part 2.

	ceive	pose	vise

1.   super + _____ + or = _____
                              = a boss

2.   con + _____ + able = _____
                              = possible, thinkable

3.   ex + _____ + ed = _____
                          = uncovered

Part 3.

1.   _____ + _____ = _____

2.   _____ + _____ = _____

3.   _____ + _____ = _____

Part 4.

1. _____   2. _____

3. _____   4. _____

5. _____   6. _____

Part 5.

1.   in + struct + or = _____

2.   take + ing = _____

3.   re + cept + ion = _____

4.   tele + vise + ion = _____

5.   deny + al = _____

6.   blot + er = _____

7.   mad + ness = _____

8.   ship + ment = _____

Part 6.

1. _____   2. _____

3. _____   4. _____

5. _____   6. _____

Part 7.

1. _____   2. _____

3. _____   4. _____

5. _____   6. _____

7. _____   8. _____

9. _____   10. _____

11. _____   12. _____

Apples and Pears

Part 8.

1. _____
   _____

2. _____
   _____

3. _____
   _____

4. _____
   _____

Apples and Pears

Date: _____

Part 1.

1. com + pute + er = _____

2. re + pute + ate + ion = _____

3. de + pute + y = _____

Part 2.

1. If your team leader is away, you will act as his

   _____ .

2. How many games do you have for your

   _____ ?

3. If you study hard, you will get a good

   _____ .

Part 3.

1. _____ + _____ + _____ = disputed

2. _____ + _____ + _____ = physically

3. _____ + _____ + _____ = photographic

4. _____ + _____ + _____ = supposed

5. _____ + _____ + _____ = received

6. _____ + _____ + _____ = acceptable

7. _____ + _____ + _____ = rebuilding

8. _____ + _____ + _____ = retractable

Part 3. Continued.

1. _____   2. _____

3. _____   4. _____

5. _____   6. _____

7. _____   8. _____

Part 4.

1. _____   2. _____

3. _____

Part 5.

1. Would you take these registers to the Deputy Heads office?

2. German generals don't often have ginger hair.

3. I imagine you would like to use your brothers computer.

1. _____

   _____

2. _____

   _____

3. _____

   _____

Apples and Pears

Part 6.

1. arm + y = _____

2. pity + ed = _____

3. set + ing = _____

4. worry + ing = _____

5. en + joy + able = _____

6. dis + pose + al = _____

7. re + serve + ing = _____

8. con + tract + ion = _____

Part 7.

1. _____ 2. _____

3. _____ 4. _____

5. _____ 6. _____

7. _____ 8. _____

9. _____ 10. _____

11. _____ 12. _____

Part 8.

1. _____
_____

2. _____
_____

3. _____
_____

Apples and Pears

Date: _____

Part 1.

Match these contractions to their meanings.

should've •   • would have

would've •   • could have

could've •   • should have

Rewrite these sentences using the contractions above.

1. We could have left on Monday.

   _____

   _____

2. I would have done my homework if I could have found a pencil.

   _____

   _____

3. They should have been here on time.

   _____

   _____

Part 2.

Part 3.

1. _____
   _____

2. _____
   _____

3. _____
   _____

4. _____
   _____

5. _____
   _____

6. _____
   _____

7. _____
   _____

8. _____
   _____

9. _____
   _____

10. _____
   _____

11. _____
   _____

12. _____
   _____

Apples and Pears

Date: _____

Part 1.

Match the following words to their meanings.

deputy •   • get rid of

dispose •   • changing, studying

revising •   • someone who acts for
                            the boss

Part 2.

1. image + ine + ate + ion = _____
2. super + vise + or = _____
3. dis + pute + ed = _____
4. im + pound + ed = _____
5. un + register + ed = _____
6. mage + ic = _____

1. _____   2. _____

3. _____   4. _____

5. _____   6. _____

Part 3.

1. _____

_____

2. _____

_____

3. _____

_____

Part 4.

Write the words in alphabetical order.

mobile	1. _____
physic	2. _____
general	3. _____
imagine	4. _____
phone	5. _____
rely	6. _____
busy	7. _____
deny	8. _____

Part 5.

1. _____	2. _____
3. _____	4. _____
5. _____	6. _____
7. _____	8. _____
9. _____	10. _____
11. _____	12. _____
13. _____	14. _____
15. _____	16. _____
17. _____	18. _____
19. _____	20. _____
21. _____	22. _____
23. _____	24. _____

Part 6.

Insert **its** or **it's**.

it's - it is
its - belongs to it

1. _____ too early to put up notices for the dance next weekend.

2. The huge brown horse lost _____ chance to jump the fence.

3. _____ time to search for some moist earth to plant these seeds in.

1. _____

_____

2. _____

_____

3. _____

_____

Part 7.

Add the morphemes in each box to find the words that fit into the grid.

| super + vise + or |
| dive + er | droop |
| use + er + s |
| tax + es | sure + er |
| un + dis + pute + ed |

u	n							
	■		■		■	■		■
	■		■		■	■		■
	■		■		■	■		■

Apples and Pears

Date: _____

Part 1.

1. un + ne + cess + ary = _____

2. suc + cess + ful = _____

3. ac + cess = _____

Part 2.

1. They were denied _____ to the secret room.

2. I hate doing _____ work.

3. A _____ business man makes a lot of money.

Part 3.

1. _____ + _____ + _____ = recession

2. _____ + _____ + _____ = imaginary

3. _____ + _____ + _____ = successive

4. _____ + _____ + _____ = television

5. ___ + _____ + _____ + ___ = necessarily

6. ___ + _____ + _____ + ___ = unsupervised

7. _____ + _____ = immobile

8. _____ + _____ + _____ = physically

1. _____ 2. _____

3. _____ 4. _____

5. _____ 6. _____

7. _____ 8. _____

Part 4.

1. _____   2. _____

3. _____

Part 5.

1. Can you guess the _____ of that big brown
   (weight, wait)
   _____ ?
   (bear, bare)

2. I'd love to eat a _____ of that gingerbread.
   (peace, piece)

3. Last _____ we flew on a _____ to Germany.
   (weak, week)   (plain, plane)

weight - how heavy it is wait - sit around	bare - uncovered bear - a teddy	piece - a bit of it peace - not fighting
week - seven days weak - not strong	plain - ordinary plane - a flying machine	

1. _____

   _____

2. _____

   _____

3. _____

   _____

Part 6.

1. re + vise + ing = _____

2. physic + s = _____

3. watch + ing = _____

4. hurry + ing = _____

5. ob + serve + er = _____

6. climb + ing = _____

7. copy + er = _____

8. step + ing = _____

Part 7.

1. _____ 2. _____

3. _____ 4. _____

5. _____ 6. _____

7. _____ 8. _____

9. _____ 10. _____

11. _____ 12. _____

Part 8.

1. _____

_____

2. _____

_____

3. _____

_____

Apples and Pears

Date: _____

Part 1.

1. _____ 2. _____

3. _____ 4. _____

5. _____ 6. _____

Part 2.

1.   dis + guise + ed = _____

2.   pro + cess + ing = _____

3.   de + pute + y = _____

Part 3.

| pute | ceive | vise |

1. in + con + _____ + able = _____
   = unthinkable

2. di + _____ + ion = _____
   = part of an army

3. dis + _____ + ed = _____
   = argued

Part 4.

1.   radio + act + ive = _____

2.   com + pute + er + s = _____

3.   re + vise + ion = _____

4.   physic + s = _____

5.   play + ing = _____

6.   be + cause = _____

7.   guilt + y = _____

8.   real + ly = _____

Apples and Pears

Part 5.

1. _____ + _____ + _____ = _____

2. ____ + _____ + _____ + _____ = _____

3. _____ + _____ + _____ = _____

Part 6.

1. _____ 2. _____

3. _____ 4. _____

5. _____ 6. _____

Part 7.

1. _____ 2. _____

3. _____ 4. _____

5. _____ 6. _____

7. _____ 8. _____

9. _____ 10. _____

11. _____ 12. _____

Part 8.

1. _____

   _____

2. _____

   _____

3. _____

   _____

4. _____

   _____

Apples and Pears

Date: _____

Part 1.

1. re + ply + ed = _____

2. ap + ply + ing = _____

3. sup + ply + ed = _____

Part 2.

1. My mother is _____ for a job selling computers.

2. Have you _____ to that letter from your grandmother?

3. The spare parts were _____ by the car dealer.

Part 3.

1. _____ + _____ + _____ = implied

2. _____ + _____ + _____ = compliance

3. _____ + _____ = telescope

4. ____ + _____ + _____ + ____ = successfully

5. _____ + _____ + _____ = receiver

6. _____ + _____ + _____ = composer

7. ____ + _____ + _____ + ____ = reputation

8. ____ + _____ + _____ + ____ = necessarily

Part 4.

1. Have you replied to your uncles letters?

2. Does she enjoy playing her brothers guitar?

3. Our guide took us around seven different churches.

Part 4. Continued.

1. _____
   _____

2. _____
   _____

3. _____
   _____

Part 5.

1. _____   2. _____

3. _____

Part 6.

1.   com + ply + es = _____

2.   suc + cess + ive = _____

3.   dis + guise + ed = _____

4.   grand + mother = _____

5.   pro + pose + al = _____

6.   phone + ed = _____

7. image + ine + ate + ion = _____

8.   re + pute + ate + ion = _____

1. _____   2. _____

3. _____   4. _____

5. _____   6. _____

7. _____   8. _____

Apples and Pears

Part 7.

1. _____
2. _____
3. _____
4. _____
5. _____
6. _____
7. _____
8. _____
9. _____
10. _____
11. _____
12. _____

Part 8.

1. _____
_____

2. _____
_____

3. _____
_____

Part 9.

1. _____
_____

Apples and Pears

Date: _____

Part 1.

Match the following words to their meanings.

complied •　　　　• easy to get to

accessible •　　　　• followed the rules

replied •　　　　• answered

Part 2.

1. ap + ply + es = _____
2. ne + cess + ary = _____
3. learn + ing = _____
4. im + ply + ed = _____
5. suc + cess = _____
6. mage + ic = _____
7. image + ine + ary = _____
8. guilt + y = _____

1. _____ 2. _____

3. _____ 4. _____

5. _____ 6. _____

7. _____ 8. _____

Part 3.

1. _____

_____

2. _____

_____

3. _____

_____

Apples and Pears

Part 4.

Write the words in alphabetical order.

radio

guest

business

thumb

freight

dawn

known

price

1. _____

2. _____

3. _____

4. _____

5. _____

6. _____

7. _____

8. _____

Part 5.

1. _____
2. _____
3. _____
4. _____
5. _____
6. _____
7. _____
8. _____
9. _____
10. _____
11. _____
12. _____
13. _____
14. _____
15. _____
16. _____
17. _____
18. _____
19. _____
20. _____
21. _____
22. _____
23. _____
24. _____

Part 6.

there - in that place, there is, there are they're - they are their - belongs to them

1. _____ are several cute young women standing by the door.

2. Policewomen must always wear _____ badges.

3. I don't know why _____ scared of our dog.

1. _____

   _____

2. _____

   _____

3. _____

   _____

Part 7.

Arrange the words in the square so that it reads the same down and across.

lull
ugly
glue
yell

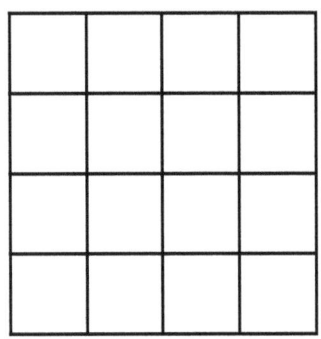

Apples and Pears

Date: _____

Part 1.

All of the word sums that end in **doubling morphemes** are circled.

per + (mit)   dis + pute   ob + ject   pro + (pel)

con + (trol)   trans + port   un + (snap)   sup + ply

Part 2.

1. _____ + _____ = repel
2. _____ + _____ = impose
3. _____ + _____ = commit
4. _____ + _____ = contract

Part 3.

1. permit + ed = permitted
2. commit + ee = committee
3. object + ed = objected
4. commit + ment = commitment
5. propel + er = propeller
6. transship + ment = transshipment

Part 4.

1. sub + mit + ing = _____
2. for + got + en = _____
3. for + get + ful = _____
4. con + fess + ing = _____
5. con + trol + er = _____
6. re + vise + ing = _____
7. pro + fit + less = _____
8. re + ject + ed = _____

27

Apples and Pears

Part 5.

1. per + mit + ed = permitted

2. _____ + _____ + _____ = dispelling

3. _____ + _____ + _____ = forgetting

4. _____ + _____ + _____ + _____ = objectionable

5. _____ + _____ + _____ = regrettable

6. _____ + _____ + _____ = proposer

Part 6.

1. I would've been here sooner if I hadn't forgotten my bus fare.

   _____

   _____

2. Let's see how we could've prevented those rabbits from getting into your garden.

   _____

   _____

3. I'll scream very loudly if you don't let me have another piece of cake.

   _____

   _____

4. They're the people who should've kept the donkeys off the lawn.

   _____

   _____

Part 6. Continued:

5. You won't be admitted if you aren't wearing a dress.

_____

_____

6. You would've regretted it, if you'd missed my birthday party.

_____

_____

7. There won't be any swans left if you aren't more careful with that rifle.

_____

_____

8. I wouldn't have permitted him to leave with the computer if he hadn't paid enough money.

_____

_____

Apples and Pears

Date: _____

Part 1.

1.   com + mit + ment = _____

2.   per + mit + ed = _____

3.   trans + mit + er = _____

Part 2.

1. Cell phones are not _____ in this building.

2. We have just bought a powerful radio

_____ .

3. Buying a puppy or a kitten is a serious

_____ .

Part 3.

1.   _____ + _____ + _____ = permitted

2.   _____ + _____ + _____ = regrettable

3.   _____ + _____ + _____ = supplied

4.   _____ + _____ + _____ = forgotten

5.   _____ + _____ + _____ = transshipment

6.   _____ + _____ + _____ = television

7. _____ + _____ + _____ + _____ + ____
= exceptionally

8.   _____ + _____ + _____ = submitting

1. _____   2. _____

3. _____   4. _____

5. _____   6. _____

7. _____   8. _____

Part 4.

1. _____ 2. _____

3. _____

Part 5.

1. Do you want your present _____ ?
   (wrapped, rapped)

2. My brother got so angry that he _____ a book at the television.
   (threw, through)

3. You must pay your _____ to the driver.
   (fair, fare)

wrap - cover with paper	threw - tossed in the air	fair - 'It's not fair!'
rap - a loud noise	through - in one side and out the other	fare - what you pay for a bus ride

1. _____

_____

2. _____

_____

3. _____

_____

Apples and Pears

Part 6.

1. for + get + ful = _____

2. point + less = _____

3. sub + mit + ing = _____

4. grand + mother = _____

5. in + struct + or = _____

6. ex + cept + ion + al + ly = _____

7. study + es = _____

8. angry + ly = _____

Part 7.

1. _____   2. _____

3. _____   4. _____

5. _____   6. _____

7. _____   8. _____

9. _____   10. _____

11. _____   12. _____

Part 8.

1. _____

_____

2. _____

_____

3. _____

_____

Apples and Pears

First Trial *Date:* _____

1. _____   2. _____

3. _____   4. _____

5. _____   6. _____

7. _____   8. _____

9. _____   10. _____

11. _____   12. _____

13. _____   14. _____

15. _____   16. _____

17. _____   18. _____

19. _____   20. _____

Second Trial *Date:* _____

1. _____   2. _____

3. _____   4. _____

5. _____   6. _____

7. _____   8. _____

9. _____   10. _____

11. _____   12. _____

13. _____   14. _____

15. _____   16. _____

17. _____   18. _____

19. _____   20. _____

Apples and Pears

Date: _____

Part 1.

1. _____   2. _____

3. _____   4. _____

5. _____   6. _____

Part 2.

1.   dis + sign + er = _____

2.   beauty + ful = _____

3.   un + trouble + ed = _____

Part 3.

	pose	tract	mit

1.   per + _____ + ed = _____
      = allowed

2.   pro + _____ + al = _____
      = a plan

3.   re + _____ + ed = _____
      = pulled back

Part 4.

1.   _____ + _____ + _____ = _____

2.   _____ + _____ + _____ = _____

3.   _____ + _____ + _____ = _____

Part 5.

1. _____   2. _____

3. _____   4. _____

5. _____   6. _____

Part 6.

1.   re + sign + ed = _____

2.   worry + ed = _____

3.   beauty + ful = _____

4.   plan + ing = _____

5.   com + mit + ee = _____

6.   list + en = _____

Part 7.

1. _____   2. _____

3. _____   4. _____

5. _____   6. _____

7. _____   8. _____

9. _____   10. _____

11. _____   12. _____

Part 8.

1. _____

_____

2. _____

_____

3. _____

_____

4. _____

_____

Apples and Pears

Date: _____

Part 1.

1.   fail + ure = _____

2.   please + ure = _____

3.   text + ure = _____

Part 2.

1. I don't like the scratchy _____ of a woolen sweater.

2. If I don't pass my exams, everyone will think I'm a _____ .

3. Do you really get that much _____ from watching television?

Part 3.

1.   _____ + _____ = gesture

2.   _____ + _____ + _____ = transmitting

3.   _____ + _____ + _____ = compliance

4.   _____ + _____ + _____ = appliance

5.   _____ + _____ + _____ = necessary

6.   _____ + _____ = pressure

7.   _____ + _____ + _____ = featuring

8. ____ + _____ + _____ + _____ = receptionist

1. _____   2. _____

3. _____   4. _____

5. _____   6. _____

7. _____   8. _____

Apples and Pears

Part 4.

1. _____   2. _____

3. _____

Part 5.

1. My sisters ideas are always getting us into trouble.

2. Those new designs are really beautiful.

3. You ought to listen to your teachers lesson.

1. _____

_____

2. _____

_____

3. _____

_____

Part 6.

1.   please + ure + able = _____

2.   tire + some = _____

3.   froze + en = _____

4.   re + ceive + ed = _____

5.   con + sign + ment = _____

6.   com + mit + ee = _____

7.   press + ure = _____

8.   ap + ply + ance + s = _____

Part 7.

1. _____ 2. _____

3. _____ 4. _____

5. _____ 6. _____

7. _____ 8. _____

9. _____ 10. _____

11. _____ 12. _____

Part 8.

1. _____

   _____

2. _____

   _____

3. _____

   _____

Apples and Pears

Date: _____

1. _____
   _____

2. _____
   _____

3. _____
   _____

4. _____
   _____

5. _____
   _____

6. _____
   _____

7. _____
   _____

8. _____
   _____

9. _____
   _____

10. _____
   _____

11. _____
   _____

12. _____
   _____

Apples and Pears

Date: _____

Part 1.

Match the following words to their meanings.

texture •   • it sends radio signals

transmitter •   • obeyed; handed in

submitted •   • how it feels

Part 2.

1.   ap + ply + ance = _____

2.   list + en = _____

3.   suc + cess + ful = _____

4.   study + es = _____

5.   press + ure = _____

6.   sup + pose + ed = _____

7.   per + mit + ed = _____

8.   pay + ing = _____

1. _____   2. _____

3. _____   4. _____

5. _____   6. _____

7. _____   8. _____

Part 3.

1. _____

_____

2. _____

_____

3. _____

_____

Apples and Pears

Part 4.

Write the words in alphabetical order.

listen

sign

great

beauty

idea

trouble

failure

magic

1. _____

2. _____

3. _____

4. _____

5. _____

6. _____

7. _____

8. _____

Part 5.

1. _____

2. _____

3. _____

4. _____

5. _____

6. _____

7. _____

8. _____

9. _____

10. _____

11. _____

12. _____

13. _____

14. _____

15. _____

16. _____

17. _____

18. _____

19. _____

20. _____

21. _____

22. _____

23. _____

24. _____

Part 6.

1. We might go hiking this morning, but _____ still not certain.

2. I'd like to build a bridge but _____ too difficult for me.

3. _____ been a real pleasure, playing that beautiful tune.

> it's - it is, it has
> its - belongs to it

1. _____

_____

2. _____

_____

3. _____

_____

Part 7.

Add the morphemes in each box to find the words that fit into the grid.

| re + ceive + er |

| muse + ic | | cover |

| com + ply + ance |

| ever + y | | never |

| vise + ion |

(grid with letters i o n)

Apples and Pears

Date: _____

Part 1.

1.   com + pel + ed = _____

2.   pro + pel + er = _____

3.   ex + pel + ed = _____

Part 2.

1. He was _____ from school for making rude gestures.

2. A ship's _____ drives it through the water.

3. In days gone by, slaves were _____ to work for their masters.

Part 3.

1.   _____ + _____ + _____ = textured

2.   _____ + _____ + _____ = repellent

3.   _____ + _____ + _____ = disposal

4.   _____ + _____ + _____ = implied

5.   _____ + _____ = reliance

1. _____   2. _____

3. _____   4. _____

5. _____

Part 4.

1. _____   2. _____

3. _____

Apples and Pears

Part 5.

1. I _____ your bright idea would be a failure.
   (knew, new)

2. If you get into any trouble, just _____ on my door.
   (rap, wrap)

3. He drove _____ the city center without stopping.
   (threw, through)

wrap - cover with paper	threw - tossed in the air	new - not old
rap - a loud noise	through - in one side and out the other	knew - what you were sure of

1. _____

   _____

2. _____

   _____

3. _____

   _____

Part 6.

1. un + please + ant = _____

2. in + sect = _____

3. re + vise = _____

4. sub + mit + ed = _____

5. pro + ject = _____

6. ex + pose + ed = _____

7. re + pel + ent = _____

8. press + ure = _____

Apples and Pears

Part 7.

1. _____ 2. _____

3. _____ 4. _____

5. _____ 6. _____

7. _____ 8. _____

9. _____ 10. _____

11. _____ 12. _____

Part 8.

1. _____

_____

2. _____

_____

3. _____

_____

Date: _____

Part 1.

1. _____ 2. _____

3. _____ 4. _____

5. _____ 6. _____

Part 2.

1.   un + nate + ure + al = _____

2.   measure + ment = _____

3.   future + ist + ic = _____

Part 3.

        ply   sign   pel

1.   com + _____ + ed = _____
                             = forced

2.   im + _____ + ed = _____
                             = hinted

3.   re + _____ + ing = _____
                             = quitting

Part 4.

1.   _____ + _____ + _____ = _____

2.   ____ + _____ + ____ + _____ = _____

3.   _____ + _____ = _____

Part 5.

1. _____ 2. _____

3. _____ 4. _____

5. _____ 6. _____

Part 6.

1. com + ply = _____

2. com + pute + er = _____

3. hid + en = _____

4. measure + ed = _____

5. un + suc + cess + ful = _____

6. busy + ness = _____

7. un + ne + cess + ary = _____

Part 7.

1. _____   2. _____

3. _____   4. _____

5. _____   6. _____

7. _____   8. _____

9. _____   10. _____

11. _____   12. _____

Part 8.

1. _____

_____

2. _____

_____

3. _____

_____

4. _____

_____

Apples and Pears

Date: _____

Part 1.

1.   in + tend + ed = _____

2.   pre + tend + ing = _____

3.   ex + tend = _____

Part 2.

1. When I am wearing this disguise, I am _____ to be a swan.

2. You will have to _____ the ladder to reach the roof.

3. We _____ to go early this morning, but we were delayed.

Part 3.

1. _____ + _____ + _____ + _____ = contenders

2. _____ + _____ + _____ = attractive

3. _____ + _____ = station

4. ____ + _____ + _____ + _____ = objectively

5. _____ + _____ + _____ = entertainment

6. _____ + _____ + _____ = constructive

7. _____ + _____ + _____ = deserving

8. _____ + _____ + _____ = accepting

1. _____   2. _____

3. _____   4. _____

5. _____   6. _____

7. _____   8. _____

Part 4.

1. _____   2. _____

3. _____

Part 5.

1. It's a cats nature to catch mice and small birds.

2. Which teams are top contenders to reach the Cup Final?

3. He is serving time at the Queens pleasure.

1. _____

_____

2. _____

_____

3. _____

_____

Part 6.

1.   measure + ment + s   = _____

2.   nate + ure + al   = _____

3.   de + sign + ing   = _____

4.   take + en   = _____

5.   in + sect   = _____

6.   suc + cess + ful   = _____

7.   de + vise + ed   = _____

8.   re + pel + ent   = _____

Apples and Pears

Part 7.

1. _____   2. _____

3. _____   4. _____

5. _____   6. _____

7. _____   8. _____

9. _____   10. _____

11. _____   12. _____

Part 8.

1. _____

_____

2. _____

_____

3. _____

_____

Date: _____

Part 1.

Match the following words to their meanings.

extended •   • fight off

expelled •   • made longer

repel •   • threw out

Part 2.

1.   treasure + y = _____
2.   un + in + tend + ed = _____
3.   im + mature = _____
4.   pro + pel = _____
5.   feat + ure + ing = _____
6.   un + trouble + ed = _____
7.   sign + al + s = _____
8.   com + mit + ment = _____

1. _____ 2. _____

3. _____ 4. _____

5. _____ 6. _____

7. _____ 8. _____

Part 3.

1. _____

_____

2. _____

_____

3. _____

_____

Part 4.

Write the words in alphabetical order.

pleasure

photo

pity

propel

paw

price

punch

pond

1. _____

2. _____

3. _____

4. _____

5. _____

6. _____

7. _____

8. _____

Part 5.

1. _____   2. _____

3. _____   4. _____

5. _____   6. _____

7. _____   8. _____

9. _____   10. _____

11. _____   12. _____

13. _____   14. _____

15. _____   16. _____

17. _____   18. _____

19. _____   20. _____

21. _____   22. _____

23. _____   24. _____

Apples and Pears

Part 6.

> there - in that place, there is, there are
> they're - they are
> their - belongs to them

1. _____ measuring up the office for the new carpet.

2. _____ ideas have a reputation for silliness.

3. Please sign your name _____ , on the dotted line.

1. _____

_____

2. _____

_____

3. _____

_____

Part 7.

1. _____

_____

Part 8.

Apples and Pears

Date: _____

Part 1.

1. ex + pire + ed = _____

2. ad + mire = _____

3. re + quire + ment + s = _____

Part 2.

1. I really _____ your beautiful pictures.

2. I think my library card has _____ .

3. What are the _____ to get into that school?

Part 3.

1. _____ + _____ + _____ = displeasure

2. _____ + _____ + _____ + _____ = overextended

3. _____ + _____ + _____ = propellant

4. _____ + _____ + _____ = appliance

5. _____ + _____ + _____ = accessible

6. ___ + _____ + _____ + _____ = reputation

7. _____ + _____ + _____ = conceivable

8. ___ + _____ + _____ + ___ + ___ = exceptionally

1. _____   2. _____

3. _____   4. _____

5. _____   6. _____

7. _____   8. _____

Part 4.

1. _____   2. _____

3. _____

Apples and Pears

Part 5.

1. Can a _____ climb a _____ tree?
   (bear , bare)   (fir , fur)

2. We had to _____ for _____ _____ .
   (weight , wait)   (ate , eight)   (ours , hours)

3. Who _____ away the _____ from their
   (threw, through)   (rappings , wrappings)
   chips?

weight - how heavy it is	bare - uncovered	ate - had some food
wait - sit around	bear - an animal	eight - a number
wrap - cover with paper	threw - tossed in the air	our - belongs to us
rap - a loud noise	through - in one side and out the other	hour - 60 minutes

1. _____

   _____

2. _____

   _____

3. _____

   _____

Part 6.

1. con + duct = _____

2. sup + ply + ed = _____

3. in + quire + y = _____

4. um + pire = _____

5. treasure + er = _____

6. ac + quire = _____

7. de + pute + y = _____

8. pre + tend + ing = _____

Part 7.

1. _____

2. _____

3. _____

4. _____

5. _____

6. _____

7. _____

8. _____

9. _____

10. _____

11. _____

12. _____

Part 8.

1. _____

_____

2. _____

_____

3. _____

_____

Apples and Pears

Level 20:

Date: _____

Part 1.

1. _____   2. _____

3. _____   4. _____

5. _____   6. _____

Part 2.

1. com + pose + ite + ion = _____

2. nate + ion + al = _____

3. dis + pose + ite + ion = _____

Part 3.

mit   ply   quire

1. ac + _____ + ed = _____
   = got

2. re + _____ + ed = _____
   = answered

3. per + _____ + ing = _____
   = allowing

Part 4.

1. ____ + _____ + ____ + ____ = _____

2. _____ + _____ + _____ = _____

3. _____ + _____ = _____

Part 5.

1. _____   2. _____

3. _____   4. _____

5. _____   6. _____

Apples and Pears

Part 6.

1.   birth + day = _____

2.   grump + y = _____

3.   vote + er = _____

4.   mis + be + have + ior = _____

5.   play + ed = _____

6.   in + act + ive = _____

7.   ob + ject + ion = _____

8.   favor + ite = _____

Part 7.

1. _____   2. _____

3. _____   4. _____

5. _____   6. _____

7. _____   8. _____

9. _____   10. _____

11. _____   12. _____

Part 8.

1. _____

   _____

2. _____

   _____

3. _____

   _____

4. _____

   _____

Apples and Pears

Masery Test:

First Trial *Date:* _____

1. _____   2. _____

3. _____   4. _____

5. _____   6. _____

7. _____   8. _____

9. _____   10. _____

11. _____   12. _____

13. _____   14. _____

15. _____   16. _____

17. _____   18. _____

19. _____   20. _____

Second Trial *Date:* _____

1. _____   2. _____

3. _____   4. _____

5. _____   6. _____

7. _____   8. _____

9. _____   10. _____

11. _____   12. _____

13. _____   14. _____

15. _____   16. _____

17. _____   18. _____

19. _____   20. _____

Apples and Pears

Date: _____

Part 1.

1. office + ial = _____

2. es + sent + ial = _____

3. cord + ial = _____

Part 2.

1. Our old friends gave us a _____ welcome.

2. If you go hiking, it is _____ to carry enough water.

3. We received an _____ notice from the council.

Part 3.

A vowel-consonant morpheme that cannot stand alone never doubles.

list + en + ing ↘ listenning wrong

list + en + ing = listening right

flat + er + ed ↘ flatterred wrong

flat + er + ed = flattered right

1. norm + al + ize = _____

2. mage + ic + al = _____

3. fast + en + er = _____

4. quake + er + ish = _____

Part 4.

1. _____ 2. _____

3. _____ 4. _____

Part 5.

1. The umpires call was hotly disputed.

2. That film features some of my favorite actors.

3. Which dealers supplied your mothers furniture?

1. _____

_____

2. _____

_____

3. _____

_____

Part 6.

1.   sup + pose + ed = _____

2.   list + en + er = _____

3.   im + part + ial = _____

4.   ne + cess + ary = _____

5.   in + quire + y = _____

6.   re + pel = _____

7.   un + com + mit + ed = _____

8. in + con + ceive + able = _____

Part 7.

1. _____   2. _____

3. _____   4. _____

5. _____   6. _____

7. _____   8. _____

9. _____   10. _____

11. _____   12. _____

Part 8.

1. _____

_____

2. _____

_____

3. _____

_____

Apples and Pears

Date: _____

Part 1.

Match the following words to their meanings.

labor •   • where ships stop

harbor •   • got; obtained

acquired •   • hard work

Part 2.

1.   favor + ite = _____
2.   im + part + ial + ly = _____
3.   pose + ite + ion = _____
4.   office + ial = _____
5.   un + de + serve + ing = _____
6.   race + ial + ly = _____
7.   nate + ion + al + ist = _____
8.   ad + mire + ed = _____

1. _____   2. _____

3. _____   4. _____

5. _____   6. _____

7. _____   8. _____

Part 3.

1. _____

_____

2. _____

_____

3. _____

_____

Apples and Pears

Part 4.

Write the words in alphabetical order.

color

labor

favor

harbor

behavior

special

umpire

admire

1. _____

2. _____

3. _____

4. _____

5. _____

6. _____

7. _____

8. _____

Part 5.

1. _____

2. _____

3. _____

4. _____

5. _____

6. _____

7. _____

8. _____

9. _____

10. _____

11. _____

12. _____

13. _____

14. _____

15. _____

16. _____

17. _____

18. _____

19. _____

20. _____

21. _____

22. _____

23. _____

24. _____

Apples and Pears

Part 6.

| you're - you are |
| your - belongs to you |

1. I think _____ listening to the wrong radio station.

2. _____ behavior is certain to get you into trouble.

3. If _____ good-natured, people will do favors for you.

1. _____

_____

2. _____

_____

3. _____

_____

Part 7.

Arrange the words in the square so that it reads the same down and across.

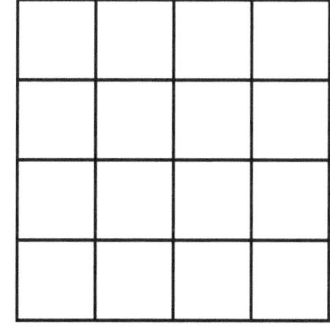

kelp
ague
rank

Apples and Pears

Level 23:

Date: _____

1. _____
   _____

2. _____
   _____

3. _____
   _____

4. _____
   _____

5. _____
   _____

6. _____
   _____

7. _____
   _____

8. _____
   _____

9. _____
   _____

10. _____
    _____

11. _____
    _____

12. _____
    _____

Apples and Pears

Date: _____

Part 1.

1. de + cise + ion = _____
2. sub + stant + ial = _____
3. exer + cise = _____

Part 2.

1. The umpire's _____ is always final.
2. To stay healthy, you need a lot of physical

   _____ .

3. They serve very _____ portions of fries.

Part 3.

1. _____ + _____ + _____ = precision
2. _____ + _____ = constant
3. _____ + _____ + _____ = decisive
4. _____ + _____ + _____ = fastening
5. _____ + _____ = concise
6. ____ + _____ + _____ + ____ = essentially
7. _____ + _____ + _____ = inquiry
8. _____ + _____ = compel

1. _____ 2. _____

3. _____ 4. _____

5. _____ 6. _____

7. _____ 8. _____

Part 4.

1. _____ 2. _____

3. _____

Part 5.

1. I think I'll _____ my favorite shirt today.
   (wear , where)

2. Maybe I'll have a bit of _____ if I hide in this
   (peace , piece)

   _____ .
   (whole , hole)

3. Do you think it's _____ to _____ a _____ coat?
   (right , write) (wear , where) (fir , fur)

wear - put clothes on	whole - all of it	piece - a bit of it
where - in what place	hole - dug with a spade	peace - not fighting
write - use a pencil	fur - animal hair	
right - correct	fir - a tree	

1. _____

_____

2. _____

_____

3. _____

_____

Part 6.

1. exer + cise + ing = _____

2. race + ial = _____

3. pre + cise + ly = _____

4. con + stant + ly = _____

5. de + cise + ion = _____

6. measure + ment = _____

7. ex + pel = _____

8. ac + cess + ible = _____

Apples and Pears

Part 7.

1. _____ 2. _____

3. _____ 4. _____

5. _____ 6. _____

7. _____ 8. _____

9. _____ 10. _____

11. _____ 12. _____

Part 8.

1. _____

_____

2. _____

_____

3. _____

_____

Apples and Pears

Date: _____

Part 1.

1. _____ 2. _____

3. _____ 4. _____

5. _____ 6. _____

Part 2.

1.   re + tire + ment = _____

2.   un + suit + able = _____

3.   en + tire + ly = _____

4.   in + cise + ion = _____

5.   im + pel + ed = _____

6.   re + ply + ed = _____

7.   dis + please + ure = _____

8.   ne + cess + ary + ly = _____

Part 3.

cord   cise   stant

1.   di + _____ = _____
                    = far away

2.   pre + _____ + ly = _____
                          = exactly

3.   _____ + ial = _____
                      = friendly

Part 4.

1. _____ + _____ + _____ = _____

2. _____ + _____ + _____ = _____

3. _____ + _____ + _____ = _____

Part 5.

1. _____   2. _____

3. _____   4. _____

5. _____   6. _____

Part 6.

1. cord + ial + ly = _____

2. spill + ed = _____

3. re + tire + ment = _____

4. re + ply + ed = _____

5. strange + er = _____

6. grand + father = _____

7. treasure + y = _____

8. un + nate + ure + al = _____

Part 7.

1. _____   2. _____

3. _____   4. _____

5. _____   6. _____

7. _____   8. _____

9. _____   10. _____

11. _____   12. _____

Part 8.

1. _____

_____

2. _____

_____

3. _____

_____

Apples and Pears

Date: _____

Part 1.

1.   per + fect = _____

2.   de + fect + ive = _____

3. af + fect + ion + ate = _____

Part 2.

1. Our new kitten is very _____ .

2. I got a _____ score in our English test.

3. We had to send the computer back because it was

_____.

Part 3.

1.   _____ + _____ + _____ = incision

2. _____ + _____ + _____ + _____ = insubstantial

3. _____ + _____ + _____ + _____ = effectively

4.   _____ + _____ + _____ = precisely

5.   _____ + _____ + _____ = globalism

6.   _____ + _____ + _____ = pretending

7.   _____ + _____ + _____ = compelled

8.   _____ + _____ + _____ = featuring

1. _____ 2. _____

3. _____ 4. _____

5. _____ 6. _____

7. _____ 8. _____

Part 4.

1. _____   2. _____

3. _____

Part 5.

1. The strangers suit was dark blue.

2. Bare wires should be left strictly alone.

3. My sisters favorite drink is apple juice.

1. _____

_____

2. _____

_____

3. _____

_____

Part 6.

1.   in + fect + ious   = _____

2.   per + fect   = _____

3.   mage+ ic + al   = _____

4.   physic + al   = _____

5.   sub + stant + ial   = _____

6.   de + sign + er   = _____

7.   beauty + ful   = _____

8.   trouble + some   = _____

9.   high + ly   = _____

Apples and Pears

Part 7.

1. _____   2. _____

3. _____   4. _____

5. _____   6. _____

7. _____   8. _____

9. _____   10. _____

11. _____   12. _____

Part 8.

1. _____

_____

2. _____

_____

3. _____

_____

Apples and Pears

Date: _____

Part 1.

Match the following words to their meanings.

precisely •   • at once

labor •   • exactly

instantly •   • work

Part 2.

1. nag + ing = _____

2. re + cept + ion = _____

3. dis + in + fect + ant = _____

4. wed + ing = _____

5. con + stant + ly = _____

6. study + es = _____

7. suit + able = _____

8. at + tend = _____

1. _____ 2. _____

3. _____ 4. _____

5. _____ 6. _____

7. _____ 8. _____

Part 3.

1. _____

_____

2. _____

_____

3. _____

_____

Apples and Pears

Part 4.

Write the words in alphabetical order.

guilt

guest

great

juice

suit

wire

tire

favor

1. _____

2. _____

3. _____

4. _____

5. _____

6. _____

7. _____

8. _____

Part 5.

1. _____

2. _____

3. _____

4. _____

5. _____

6. _____

7. _____

8. _____

9. _____

10. _____

11. _____

12. _____

13. _____

14. _____

15. _____

16. _____

17. _____

18. _____

19. _____

20. _____

21. _____

22. _____

23. _____

24. _____

Part 6.

| it's - it is |
| its - belongs to it |

1. A dog shows _____ displeasure by baring _____ teeth.

2. If it barks, _____ certainly not a cat.

3. I think _____ time to retire to bed.

1. _____

_____

2. _____

_____

3. _____

_____

Part 7.

1. _____

_____

Part 8.

Add the morphemes in each box to find the words that fit into the grid.

| re + nove + ate + ion |
office + ial + ly	art
civic	fine + al
oar + ed	yen
de + lect + able	oil

Apples and Pears

Date: _____

Part 1.

1.   pro + duce = _____

2.   re + duce + ing = _____

3.   intro + duce + ed = _____

Part 2.

1. A cow can _____ enough milk for ten people.

2. Have you _____ your friends to your mother?

3. If you are serious about _____ your weight, you must eat less.

Part 3.

1. _____ + _____ + _____ + _____ = effectively

2. _____ + _____ + _____ = conducive

3. _____ + _____ + _____ = precision

4. _____ + _____ = distant

5. _____ + _____ + _____ + _____ = impartially

6. _____ + _____ + _____ = requirement

7. _____ + _____ + _____ = tendering

8. _____ + _____ + _____ = featuring

1. _____   2. _____

3. _____   4. _____

5. _____   6. _____

7. _____   8. _____

Apples and Pears

Part 4.

1. _____ 2. _____

3. _____

Part 5.

1. I thought you _____ that we were _____ to
   (new , knew)   (through , threw)
   the final.

2. Who burned the _____ on that poor dog's _____?
   (fur , fir)   (tail , tale)

3. The stranger said that he _____ _____ us _____ .
   (wood , would) (meet , meat) (here , hear)

knew - what you thought	threw - tossed in the air	tail - dogs wag them
new - not old	through - in one side and out the other	tale - a story
would - might do it	meet - get together	fur - animal hair
wood - comes from trees	meat - something to eat	fir - a tree
hear - with your ears		
here - in this place		

1. _____

   _____

2. _____

   _____

3. _____

   _____

Part 6.

1.   exer + cise = _____

2.   con + duce + ive = _____

3.   beauty + ful = _____

4.   re + duce = _____

5.   tele + vise + ion = _____

Part 6. Continued.

6.   intro + duce = _____

7.   sup + ply + es = _____

8.   physic + al = _____

Part 7.

1. _____   2. _____

3. _____   4. _____

5. _____   6. _____

7. _____   8. _____

9. _____   10. _____

11. _____   12. _____

Part 8.

1. _____

_____

2. _____

_____

3. _____

_____

Apples and Pears

Date: _____

Part 1.

1. _____   2. _____

3. _____   4. _____

5. _____   6. _____

Part 2.

1.   dis + con + tinue + ed = _____

2.   per + fect + ion = _____

3.   con + stant + ly = _____

4.   exer + cise + ing = _____

5.   pro + cess + ion = _____

6.   ex + pel + ing = _____

7.   plenty + ful = _____

8.   ad + mire + ing = _____

Part 3.

        tend   part   duce

1.   pro + _____ + ing = _____
                              = making

2.   im + _____ + ial = _____
                              = fair

3.   at + _____ + ance = _____
                              = how often you show up

Part 4.

1.   _____ + _____ + _____ = _____

2.   _____ + _____ + _____ = _____

3.   _____ + _____ + _____ = _____

Part 5.

1. _____ 2. _____

3. _____ 4. _____

5. _____ 6. _____

Part 6.

1. de + sign + er = _____

2. value + able = _____

3. pro + duce + ing = _____

4. un + like + ly = _____

5. en + joy + able = _____

6. hungry + er = _____

7. tire + ed = _____

8. con + tain + er = _____

Part 7.

1. _____ 2. _____

3. _____ 4. _____

5. _____ 6. _____

7. _____ 8. _____

9. _____ 10. _____

11. _____ 12. _____

Part 8.

1. _____

_____

2. _____

_____

3. _____

_____

Apples and Pears

Date: _____

Part 1.

1. mess + age + es = _____

2. pack + age = _____

3. store + age = _____

Part 2.

1. Did you get the _____ I left on your cell phone?

2. If you aren't using that television, we should put it in _____ .

3. We received the _____ in the post.

Part 3.

1. _____ + _____ = runny

2. _____ + _____ = rescued

3. _____ + _____ + _____ = received

4. _____ + _____ + _____ = effective

5. _____ + _____ + _____ = precision

6. _____ + _____ = passage

7. _____ + _____ = official

8. ____ + _____ + _____ + _____ = undisputed

9. _____ + _____ + _____ = appliance

10. _____ + _____ + _____ + _____ = composition

Part 3. Continued.

1. _____ 2. _____

3. _____ 4. _____

5. _____ 6. _____

7. _____ 8. _____

9. _____ 10. _____

Part 4.

1. _____ 2. _____

3. _____

Part 5.

1. We gave the girls some tissues for their runny noses.

2. Have you received your fathers messages?

3. We rescued our dinners from the dog.

1. _____

_____

2. _____

_____

3. _____

_____

Apples and Pears

Part 6.

1. hijack + ed = _____
2. band + age + s = _____
3. host + age = _____
4. rescue + ed = _____
5. car + y + age = _____
6. intro + duce = _____
7. post + age = _____
8. arm + y = _____

Part 7.

1. _____ 2. _____

3. _____ 4. _____

5. _____ 6. _____

7. _____ 8. _____

9. _____ 10. _____

11. _____ 12. _____

Part 8.

1. _____

_____

2. _____

_____

3. _____

_____

Apples and Pears

First Trial *Date:* _____

1. _____   2. _____

3. _____   4. _____

5. _____   6. _____

7. _____   8. _____

9. _____   10. _____

11. _____   12. _____

13. _____   14. _____

15. _____   16. _____

17. _____   18. _____

19. _____   20. _____

Second Trial *Date:* _____

1. _____   2. _____

3. _____   4. _____

5. _____   6. _____

7. _____   8. _____

9. _____   10. _____

11. _____   12. _____

13. _____   14. _____

15. _____   16. _____

17. _____   18. _____

19. _____   20. _____

Apples and Pears

Date: _____

Part 1.

Match the following words to their meanings.

continue •   • save

rescue •   • a wide street

avenue •   • carry on

Part 2.

1.   pack + age + ing = _____

2.   re + issue + ed = _____

3.   dis + con + tinue + ed = _____

4.   af + fect + ed = _____

5.   de + cise + ion = _____

6.   class + ic + al = _____

7.   col + lect + ion = _____

8.   heave + y + er = _____

1. _____   2. _____

3. _____   4. _____

5. _____   6. _____

7. _____   8. _____

Part 3.

1. _____

_____

2. _____

_____

3. _____

_____

Part 4.

Write the words in alphabetical order.

package

passage

partial

padding

pages

panned

paid

paying

1. _____

2. _____

3. _____

4. _____

5. _____

6. _____

7. _____

8. _____

Part 5.

1. _____

2. _____

3. _____

4. _____

5. _____

6. _____

7. _____

8. _____

9. _____

10. _____

11. _____

12. _____

13. _____

14. _____

15. _____

16. _____

17. _____

18. _____

19. _____

20. _____

21. _____

22. _____

23. _____

24. _____

Part 6.

their - belongs to them
they're - they are
there - in that place

1. They'll have to live with _____ decisions.

2. _____ running a rescue home for stray donkeys.

3. _____ building _____ house over _____ .

1. _____

_____

2. _____

_____

3. _____

_____

Part 7.

1. _____

_____

Part 8.

Apples and Pears

Date: _____

Part 1.

1. in + dis + pense + able = _____

2. com + pense + ate = _____

3. ex + pense + ive = _____

Part 2.

1. Package holidays can be very _____.

2. Nothing can _____ me for the loss of my pet toad.

3. Most young people think a cell phone is

_____ .

Part 3.

1. _____ + _____ + _____ + _____ = dispensation

2. _____ + _____ + _____ = received

3. _____ + _____ + _____ + _____ = compensation

4. _____ + _____ + _____ = inducement

5. _____ + _____ + _____ = unsuitable

6. _____ + _____ + _____ = essential

7. _____ + _____ + _____ = displeasure

8. _____ + _____ + _____ = disguised

1. _____ 2. _____

3. _____ 4. _____

5. _____ 6. _____

7. _____ 8. _____

Part 4.

1. _____   2. _____

3. _____

Part 5.

1. If the _____ is nice, we can go for a _____
   (weather, whether)   (sale, sail)
   in my boat.

2. Today I received one hundred e- _____ messages.
   (mail, male)

3. _____ a pity _____ all spam.
   (its, it's)   (there, they're, their)

their - belongs to them they're - they are there - in that place	weather - usually rain whether - if mail - by post male - boy or man	sale - in a shop sail - in a boat its - belongs to it it's - it is

1. _____

_____

2. _____

_____

3. _____

_____

Part 6.

1. health + y = _____

2. stole + en = _____

3. com + pense + ate + ion = _____

4. exer + cise = _____

5. in + ex + pense + ive = _____

6. uni + verse + al + ist = _____

Apples and Pears

Part 6. Continued.

   7.   re + ceive + ed = _____

   8.   use + ed = _____

   9.   physic + ian = _____

Part 7.

1. _____   2. _____

3. _____   4. _____

5. _____   6. _____

7. _____   8. _____

9. _____   10. _____

11. _____   12. _____

Part 8.

1. _____

_____

2. _____

_____

3. _____

_____

Date: _____

1. _____
_____

2. _____
_____

3. _____
_____

4. _____
_____

5. _____
_____

6. _____
_____

7. _____
_____

8. _____
_____

9. _____
_____

10. _____
_____

11. _____
_____

12. _____
_____

Apples and Pears

Date: _____

Part 1.

1. _____ 2. _____

3. _____ 4. _____

5. _____ 6. _____

Part 2.

1. **notice + ing = noticing but notice + able = noticeable**

2. **manage + ing = managing but manage + able = manageable**

3.   re + charge + able = _____

4.   dis + charge + ing = _____

5.   trace + ed = _____

6.   trace + able = _____

7.   change + ing = _____

8.   change + able = _____

Part 3.

duce   pense   stant

1.   ex + _____ + ive = _____
                        = not cheap

2.   con + _____ = _____
                        = staying the same

3.   in + _____ + ed = _____
                        = brought about

Part 4.

1. ____ + _____ + _____ = _____

2. _____ + _____ + _____ = _____

3. ___ + ____ + _____ + _____ = _____

95

Apples and Pears

Part 5.

1. _____ 2. _____

3. _____ 4. _____

5. _____ 6. _____

Part 6.

1. in + sure + ance = _____

2. com + pense + ate + ion = _____

3. manage + able = _____

4. tract + ion = _____

5. pay + ment = _____

6. un + en + force + able = _____

7. bare + ly = _____

8. rust + y = _____

Part 7.

1. _____ 2. _____

3. _____ 4. _____

5. _____ 6. _____

7. _____ 8. _____

9. _____ 10. _____

11. _____ 12. _____

Part 8.

1. _____

_____

2. _____

_____

3. _____

_____

Part 9.

Arrange the words in the square so that it reads the same down and across.

lode
feed
edge
clef

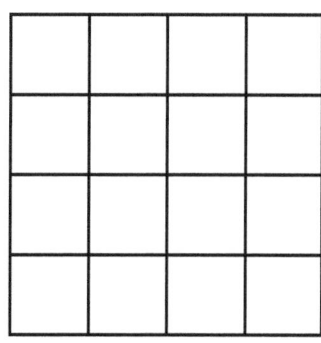

Apples and Pears

Date: _____

Part 1.

1. sup + port + er = _____

2. re + port + er = _____

3. trans + port + ate + ion = _____

Part 2.

1. Walking is the cheapest form of _____ .

2. Are you a Red Sox _____ ?

3. My uncle is a news _____ for BBC radio.

Part 3.

1. _____ + _____ + _____ = propeller

2. _____ + _____ = damaged

3. _____ + _____ + _____ = importing

4. _____ + _____ = postage

5. _____ + _____ + _____ = perfection

6. _____ + _____ + _____ = cordially

7. _____ + _____ + _____ = admitted

8. _____ + _____ + _____ = applying

1. _____   2. _____

3. _____   4. _____

5. _____   6. _____

7. _____   8. _____

Part 4.

1. _____ 2. _____

3. _____

Part 5.

1. The dog ate my fathers sausages.

2. How many cottages can they build in this village?

3. The ships propeller was damaged when it hit the reef.

1. _____

_____

2. _____

_____

3. _____

_____

Part 6.

1. es + sent + ial = _____

2. ex + pense + ive = _____

3. pack + age = _____

4. im + port = _____

5. im + pose + ing = _____

6. image + ine + ate + ion = _____

7. de + sign + er = _____

8. im + mobile + ize = _____

Part 7.

1. _____   2. _____

3. _____   4. _____

5. _____   6. _____

7. _____   8. _____

9. _____   10. _____

11. _____   12. _____

Part 8.

1. _____

_____

2. _____

_____

3. _____

_____

Apples and Pears

Date: _____

Part 1.

Match the following words to their meanings.

compensation •   • a lot of bossy people

provisions •   • makes up for a loss

committee •   • food or supplies

Part 2.

1. ex + pense + ive = _____
2. re + port + ing = _____
3. ex + port + ed = _____
4. marry + age = _____
5. change + able = _____
6. mess + age + ing = _____
7. value + able = _____
8. note + ice + able = _____

1. _____   2. _____

3. _____   4. _____

5. _____   6. _____

7. _____   8. _____

Part 3.

1. _____

_____

2. _____

_____

3. _____

_____

Apples and Pears

Part 4.

Write the words in alphabetical order.

ginger

average

juice

general

guide

suit

issue

great

wire

1. _____

2. _____

3. _____

4. _____

5. _____

6. _____

7. _____

8. _____

9. _____

Part 5.

1. _____   2. _____

3. _____   4. _____

5. _____   6. _____

7. _____   8. _____

9. _____   10. _____

11. _____   12. _____

13. _____   14. _____

15. _____   16. _____

17. _____   18. _____

19. _____   20. _____

21. _____   22. _____

23. _____   24. _____

Apples and Pears

Part 6.

| your - belongs to you |
| you're - you are |

1. If _____ afraid of ghosts, you shouldn't stay in our village.

2. Can we watch the World Cup Final on _____ television?

3. I have just received _____ text message.

1. _____

_____

2. _____

_____

3. _____

_____

Part 7.

| e + fuse + ive | elf |

| im + mature + ly |

| dive + er | gum + y |

| re + build + ing |

| in + set |

y

Apples and Pears

Date: _____

Part 1.

1.   pro + test + er + s = _____

2.   auto + graph = _____

3. auto + mate + ic + al + ly

   = _____

Part 2.

1. The television star signed her _____ in my book.

2. The _____ marched to show their objections to the war.

3. Our new microwave _____ burns your dinner.

Part 3.

1.   _____ + _____ + _____ = contested

2.   _____ + _____ + _____ = opposed

3.   _____ + _____ + _____ = automation

4.   _____ + _____ + _____ = attested

5.   _____ + _____ + _____ = rechargeable

6.   _____ + _____ + _____ = continuing

7.   _____ + _____ + _____ = untraceable

8.   _____ + _____ + _____ = packaging

1. _____ 2. _____

3. _____ 4. _____

5. _____ 6. _____

7. _____ 8. _____

Apples and Pears

Part 4.

1. _____   2. _____

3. _____

Part 5.

1. Do you know _____ _____ automobile is running?
   (weather, whether)(there, they're their)

2. Let me introduce you to Jane—she is a _____ friend.
   (deer, dear)

3. We bought some inexpensive _____ to go camping.
   (tents, tense)

their - belongs to them	weather - usually rain	tents - for camping
they're - they are	whether - if	tense - nervous, anxious
there - in that place		
	deer - it has antlers	
	dear - beloved, expensive	

1. _____

   _____

2. _____

   _____

3. _____

   _____

Part 6.

1. im + port + ant = _____

2. auto + pilot = _____

3. tele + phone = _____

4. in + vent + ion + s = _____

5. auto + mobile = _____

Part 6. Continued.

6.   fly + ing = _____

7. auto + mate + ic + al + ly

                        = _____

8.   op + pose + ite + ion = _____

9.   nate + ion + al + ize = _____

Part 7.

1. _____   2. _____

3. _____   4. _____

5. _____   6. _____

7. _____   8. _____

9. _____   10. _____

11. _____   12. _____

Part 8.

1. _____

_____

2. _____

_____

3. _____

_____

Apples and Pears

Date: _____

Part 1.

1. _____ 2. _____

3. _____ 4. _____

5. _____ 6. _____

Part 2.

1. create + ive + ly = _____

2. imit + ate + ion = _____

3. re + locate + ed = _____

4. situate + ion = _____

5. educate + ion + al + ly = _____

6. un + en + force + able = _____

7. shut + er + ed = _____

8. im + ply + ed = _____

Part 3.

struct	create	imit

1. _____ + ate + ion = _____
    = a copy

2. in + _____ + ion = _____
    = education, an order

3. re + _____ + ion = _____
    = play; leisure activity

Part 4.

1. _____ + _____ = _____

2. ___ + _____ + _____ + _____ = _____

3. ___ + _____ + _____ + _____ = _____

Apples and Pears

Part 5.

1. _____   2. _____

3. _____   4. _____

5. _____   6. _____

Part 6.

1.   sup + pose + ed = _____

2.   situate + ion = _____

3.   auto + mobile = _____

4.   in + struct + or = _____

5.   drive + ing = _____

6.   re + ceive = _____

7.   educate + ion = _____

8.   teach + es = _____

Part 7.

1. _____   2. _____

3. _____   4. _____

5. _____   6. _____

7. _____   8. _____

9. _____   10. _____

11. _____   12. _____

Part 8.

1. _____

_____

2. _____

_____

3. _____

_____

Apples and Pears

Date: _____

Part 1.

1.   dis + miss + ed = _____

2.   per + miss + ion = _____

3.   inter + miss + ion = _____

Part 2.

1. Do you have _____ to leave your seat?

2. The class will be _____ when you have finished your work.

3. We can stretch and get a drink during the

   _____ .

Part 3.

1.   _____ + _____ + _____ = protesting

2.   _____ + _____ + _____ = expensive

3.   _____ + _____ + _____ = conducive

4. _____ + _____ + _____ = unmanageable

5.   _____ + _____ = valuable

6.   _____ + _____ + _____ = precision

7.   _____ + _____ = official

8.   _____ + _____ + _____ = featuring

1. _____   2. _____

3. _____   4. _____

5. _____   6. _____

7. _____   8. _____

Part 4.

1. _____   2. _____

3. _____

Part 5.

1. Did you get the writers autograph?

2. I think I can manage at least four sausages.

3. Mothers always worry about their childrens education.

1. _____

_____

2. _____

_____

3. _____

_____

Part 6.

1.   auto + mote + ive   = _____

2.   suc + cess + ful   = _____

3.   suit + able   = _____

4.   ob + tain   = _____

5.   locate + ion   = _____

6. mote + ive + ate + ion + al

    = _____

7.   peace + able   = _____

8.   auto + mate + ion   = _____

Apples and Pears

Part 7.

1. _____ 2. _____

3. _____ 4. _____

5. _____ 6. _____

7. _____ 8. _____

9. _____ 10. _____

11. _____ 12. _____

Part 8.

1. _____

_____

2. _____

_____

3. _____

_____

Apples and Pears

Date: _____

Part 1.

Match the following words to their meanings.

repellent •   • noise; disturbance

commotion •   • off-putting; disgusting

indispensable •   • you can't do without it

Part 2.

1. un + damage + ed = _____

2. create + ive + ity = _____

3. con + tinue + ous = _____

4. fame + ous = _____

5. auto + mate + ic = _____

7. mote + ive + ate + ion = _____

7. rescue + ing = _____

8. un + note + ice + able = _____

1. _____   2. _____

3. _____   4. _____

5. _____   6. _____

7. _____   8. _____

Part 3.

1. _____

_____

2. _____

_____

3. _____

_____

Apples and Pears

Part 4.

Write the words in alphabetical order.

skill   1. _____

stretch   2. _____

switch   3. _____

scotch   4. _____

sausage   5. _____

size   6. _____

spoil   7. _____

same   8. _____

sure   9. _____

Part 5.

1. _____   2. _____

3. _____   4. _____

5. _____   6. _____

7. _____   8. _____

9. _____   10. _____

11. _____   12. _____

13. _____   14. _____

15. _____   16. _____

17. _____   18. _____

19. _____   20. _____

21. _____   22. _____

23. _____   24. _____

Apples and Pears

Part 6.

> its - belongs to it
> it's - it is

1. The white donkey can carry a huge load that is twice _____ size.

2. _____ only a cottage, but _____ still the castle of my dreams.

3. _____ time to do our stretching exercises.

1. _____

_____

2. _____

_____

3. _____

_____

Part 7.

1. _____

_____

Part 8.

Apples and Pears

First Trial *Date:* _____

1. _____   2. _____

3. _____   4. _____

5. _____   6. _____

7. _____   8. _____

9. _____   10. _____

11. _____   12. _____

13. _____   14. _____

15. _____   16. _____

17. _____   18. _____

19. _____   20. _____

Second Trial *Date:* _____

1. _____   2. _____

3. _____   4. _____

5. _____   6. _____

7. _____   8. _____

9. _____   10. _____

11. _____   12. _____

13. _____   14. _____

15. _____   16. _____

17. _____   18. _____

19. _____   20. _____

Apples and Pears

Date: _____

Part 1.

1. con + fuse + ing = _____

2. re + fuse + ed = _____

3. pro + fuse + ly = _____

Part 2.

1. All these different instructions are very

   _____ .

2. The protesters _____ to obey the police.

3. We thanked the stranger _____ for his
   kind favor.

Part 3.

1. _____ + _____ + _____ = transfusion

2. _____ + _____ + _____ + _____ = motivation

3. _____ + _____ = autopilot

4. ____ + _____ + _____ + _____ = repackaged

5. ____ + _____ + _____ + _____ = affectionate

6. _____ + _____ + _____ = decisive

7. _____ + _____ + _____ = deputy

8. _____ + _____ + _____ = opposing

1. _____   2. _____

3. _____   4. _____

5. _____   6. _____

7. _____   8. _____

Apples and Pears

Part 4.

1. _____   2. _____

3. _____

Part 5.

1. The Royal _____ is responsible for delivering the post. (Mail, Male)

2. You shouldn't _____ at him or he might get angry. (stair, stare)

3. We were very _____, _____ for the police to come. (tents, tense) (waiting, weighting)

male - boy or man	stare - look hard	tents - for camping
mail - the post	stair - you go up it	tense - nervous, anxious
wait - sit around		
weight - how heavy it is		

1. _____

_____

2. _____

_____

3. _____

_____

Part 6.

1. per + cept + ive = _____

2. con + fuse + ion = _____

3. re + mote = _____

4. locate + ion = _____

Part 6. Continued.

5.   host + age = _____

6.   deny + ed = _____

7.   copy + ing = _____

8.   rely + able = _____

Part 7.

1. _____   2. _____

3. _____   4. _____

5. _____   6. _____

7. _____   8. _____

9. _____   10. _____

11. _____   12. _____

Part 8.

1. _____

_____

2. _____

_____

3. _____

_____

Apples and Pears

Date: _____

Part 1.

1. _____ 2. _____

3. _____ 4. _____

5. _____ 6. _____

Part 2.

1. re + create + ion = _____

2. trouble + some = _____

3. image + ine + ate + ion = _____

4. mobile + ity = _____

5. sign + al = _____

6. photo + graph + ic + al + ly

   = _____

7. ne + cess + ary = _____

8. re + pute + ate + ion = _____

Part 3.

	stant	fuse	fect

1. con + _____ + ion = _____
   = a sweet

2. sub + _____ + ial = _____
   = solidly built

3. pro + _____ + ly = _____
   = generously; given freely

Apples and Pears

Part 4.

1. _____ + _____ + _____ = _____

2. _____ + _____ + _____ = _____

3. _____ + _____ + _____ = _____

Part 5.

1. _____ 2. _____

3. _____ 4. _____

5. _____ 6. _____

Part 6.

1. de + fuse + ed = _____

2. police + man = _____

3. box + er + s = _____

4. savage + ly = _____

5. situate + ion = _____

6. un + en + force + able = _____

7. create + ive + ly = _____

8. im + port + ant = _____

Part 7.

1. _____ 2. _____

3. _____ 4. _____

5. _____ 6. _____

7. _____ 8. _____

9. _____ 10. _____

11. _____ 12. _____

Part 8.

1. _____

_____

2. _____

_____

3. _____

_____

Part 9.

Arrange the words in the square so that it reads the same down and across.

neat
idea
hind
date

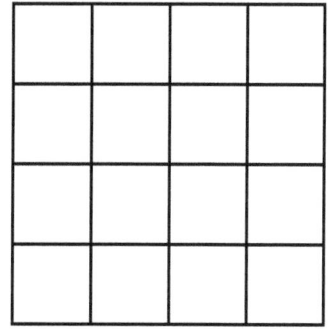

Date: _____

1. _____
   _____

2. _____
   _____

3. _____
   _____

4. _____
   _____

5. _____
   _____

6. _____
   _____

7. _____
   _____

8. _____
   _____

9. _____
   _____

10. _____
    _____

11. _____
    _____

12. _____
    _____

Apples and Pears

Date: _____

Part 1.

1. muse + ic + al + ly = _____
2. de + script + ion = _____
3. con + script + ed = _____

Part 2.

1. We gave the policeman a good _____ of the thief.
2. She is exceptionally talented _____ .
3. During the war, men were _____ into the army.

Part 3.

1. _____ + _____ + _____ = effusive
2. _____ + _____ + _____ = commotion
3. _____ + _____ + _____ = reducing
4. _____ + _____ + _____ = officially
5. _____ + _____ + _____ = propeller
6. _____ + _____ + _____ = pleasurable
7. _____ + _____ + _____ = replied
8. _____ + _____ + _____ = incessant

1. _____ 2. _____
3. _____ 4. _____
5. _____ 6. _____
7. _____ 8. _____

Part 4.

1. _____   2. _____

3. _____

Part 5.

1. We stopped Fathers subscription to the newspaper.

2. We enjoyed all the rides at the amusement park.

3. I can't stand listening to my brothers music.

1. _____

   _____

2. _____

   _____

3. _____

   _____

Part 6.

1.   com + mit + ee = _____

2.   a + muse + ing = _____

3.   pre + script + ion = _____

4.   meet + ing = _____

5.   tele + vise + ion = _____

6.   de + script + ion = _____

7.   in + fect + ion = _____

8.   script + write + er = _____

Apples and Pears

Part 7.

1. _____ 2. _____

3. _____ 4. _____

5. _____ 6. _____

7. _____ 8. _____

9. _____ 10. _____

11. _____ 12. _____

Part 8.

1. _____

_____

2. _____

_____

3. _____

_____

Date: _____

Part 1.

Match the following words to their meanings.

incessant •   • forced to join the army

inscription •   • writing

conscripted •   • it never stops

Part 2.

1.   un + muse + ic + al = _____

2.   re + locate + ed = _____

3.   re + fuse + al = _____

4.   note + ice + able = _____

5.   un + damage + ed = _____

6.   imit + ate + ion = _____

7.   oper + ate + ion = _____

8.   per + form + ed = _____

1. _____   2. _____

3. _____   4. _____

5. _____   6. _____

7. _____   8. _____

Part 3.

1. _____

_____

2. _____

_____

3. _____

_____

Part 4.

Write the words in alphabetical order.

educate 1. _____

imitate 2. _____

create 3. _____

operate 4. _____

locate 5. _____

situate 6. _____

issue 7. _____

rescue 8. _____

Part 5.

1. _____ 2. _____

3. _____ 4. _____

5. _____ 6. _____

7. _____ 8. _____

9. _____ 10. _____

11. _____ 12. _____

13. _____ 14. _____

15. _____ 16. _____

17. _____ 18. _____

19. _____ 20. _____

21. _____ 22. _____

23. _____ 24. _____

Apples and Pears

Part 6.

> their - belongs to them
> they're - they are
> there - in that place

1. _____ buying some used furniture for _____ spare room.

2. _____ grades certainly weren't very good last year.

3. _____ are several women waiting to go through.

1. _____

_____

2. _____

_____

3. _____

_____

Part 7.

Apples and Pears

Date: _____

Part 1.

1.   sub + verse + ive = _____

2.   re + verse + ed = _____

3. con + verse + ate + ion + s = _____

Part 2.

1. My mother enjoys long _____
   on the telephone.

2. My uncle _____ his car into a lamppost.

3. The spy was arrested for _____ activities.

Part 3.

1.   _____ + _____ + _____ = diversity

2.   _____ + _____ + _____ = description

3.   _____ + _____ + _____ = refusal

4. ___ + _____ + _____ + _____ + ___ = unmotivated

5.   _____ + _____ + _____ = reducing

6.   _____ + _____ = creation

7.   _____ + _____ = rescuing

8.   _____ + _____ + _____ = admitted

1. _____ 2. _____

3. _____ 4. _____

5. _____ 6. _____

7. _____ 8. _____

Part 4.

1. _____   2. _____

3. _____

Part 5.

1. The ship _____ around the propeller shaft.
   (leeks, leaks)

2. Loud music is not _____ in this village.
   (allowed, aloud)

3. The newspaper reporters would not leave the young _____ alone.
   (prints, prince)

| leak - let water in | allowed - permitted | prints - makes letters |
| leek - a vegetable | aloud - you can hear it | prince - future king |

1. _____

_____

2. _____

_____

3. _____

_____

Part 6.

1. con + verse + ate + ion + al + ist
    = _____

2. write + ing = _____

3. re + verse = _____

4. a + muse + ing = _____

5. in + script + ion = _____

Part 6. Continued.

6. grand + father = _____

7. act + ive + ity + es = _____

8. for + bid + en = _____

Part 7.

1. _____   2. _____

3. _____   4. _____

5. _____   6. _____

7. _____   8. _____

9. _____   10. _____

11. _____   12. _____

Part 8.

1. _____

_____

2. _____

_____

3. _____

_____

Apples and Pears

Date: _____

Part 1.

1. _____ 2. _____

3. _____ 4. _____

5. _____ 6. _____

Part 2.

1. ex + cept + ion + al = _____

2. ne + cess + ity + es = _____

3. at + tract + ion = _____

4. ac + count + ant = _____

5. un + reason + able = _____

6. pro + vise + ion + s = _____

7. ex + pose + ure = _____

8. op + pose + ite + ion = _____

Part 3.

	miss	muse	mate

1. a + _____ + ment = _____
    = entertainment

2. inter + _____ + ion = _____
    = a break

3. auto + _____ + ed = _____
    = it doesn't need a human operator

Part 4.

1. ____ + _____ + _____ + ____ = _____

2. _____ + _____ + _____ = _____

3. _____ + _____ = _____

Apples and Pears

Part 5.

1. _____   2. _____

3. _____   4. _____

5. _____   6. _____

Part 6.

1.   sub + script + ion = _____

2.   dis + re + pute + able = _____

3.   in + vise + ible = _____

4.   press + ure = _____

5.   ex + pire + s = _____

6.   com + ply + ance = _____

7.   re + pel + ent = _____

8.   ac + quire + ed = _____

Part 7.

1. _____   2. _____

3. _____   4. _____

5. _____   6. _____

7. _____   8. _____

9. _____   10. _____

11. _____   12. _____

Part 8.

1. _____

   _____

2. _____

   _____

3. _____

   _____

Part 9.

Apples and Pears Level 48:

Date: _____

Part 1.

1.   uni + verse + ity = _____

2.   cor + rect + s = _____

3.   di + rect + ed = _____

Part 2.

1. You don't have to go to _____ to get an education.

2. The police _____ the traffic around the wrecked cars.

3. Our teacher never _____ our spelling mistakes.

Part 3.

1.   _____ + _____ + _____ = universal

2.   _____ + _____ + _____ = diversity

3.   _____ + _____ + _____ = incorrect

4.   _____ + _____ + _____ = directive

5. _____ + _____ + _____ + _____ = redirection

6.   _____ + _____ + _____ = uniformly

7.   _____ + _____ + _____ = subversion

8.   _____ + _____ + _____ = description

1. _____ 2. _____

3. _____ 4. _____

5. _____ 6. _____

7. _____ 8. _____

Part 4.

1. _____   2. _____

3. _____

Part 5.

1. I always correct my bothers faults.

2. Does your sister have any other subversive ideas?

3. They gave us the wrong directions and we got lost.

1. _____

_____

2. _____

_____

3. _____

_____

Part 6.

1. wash + ing = _____

2. ad + mit + ed = _____

3. uni + form = _____

4. auto + mate + ic = _____

5. muse + ic + al = _____

6. trans + fuse + ion = _____

7. dis + con + tinue + ed = _____

8. re + create + ion + al = _____

Apples and Pears

Part 7.

1. _____   2. _____

3. _____   4. _____

5. _____   6. _____

7. _____   8. _____

9. _____   10. _____

11. _____   12. _____

Part 8.

1. _____

_____

2. _____

_____

3. _____

_____

Apples and Pears

Date: _____

Part 1.

Match the following words to their meanings.

uniform •   • all different

diverse •   • telling it like it is

description •   • all the same

Part 2.

1.   at + tract + ive = _____

2.   in + oper + ate + ive = _____

3.   educate + ion + al = _____

4.   de + script + ion = _____

5.   uni + verse + ity = _____

6.   act + ive + ity + es = _____

7.   dry + er = _____

8.   wash + ing = _____

1. _____   2. _____

3. _____   4. _____

5. _____   6. _____

7. _____   8. _____

Part 3.

1. _____

   _____

2. _____

   _____

3. _____

   _____

Part 4.

Write the words in alphabetical order.

autumn

August

fault

laundry

machine

tough

imitate

cottage

1. _____

2. _____

3. _____

4. _____

5. _____

6. _____

7. _____

8. _____

Part 5.

1. _____

2. _____

3. _____

4. _____

5. _____

6. _____

7. _____

8. _____

9. _____

10. _____

11. _____

12. _____

13. _____

14. _____

15. _____

16. _____

17. _____

18. _____

19. _____

20. _____

21. _____

22. _____

23. _____

24. _____

Part 6.

| your - belongs to you |
| you're - you are |

1. _____ school uniform is still in the laundry.

2. _____ smart enough to go to university if you want to.

3. This confusion is all _____ fault!

1. _____

_____

2. _____

_____

3. _____

_____

Part 7.

Arrange the words in the square so that it reads the same down and across.

wile

alas

ness

swan

Apples and Pears

Date: _____

Part 1.

  1.   ap + prove = _____

  2.   im + prove + ed = _____

  3.   di + rect + ion + s = _____

Part 2.

  1. It's amazing how much my grades _____ once I started studying.

  2. My mother doesn't _____ of my choice of music.

  3. My teacher's _____ are always confusing.

Part 3.

  1.   _____ + _____ + _____ = approval

  2.   _____ + _____ + _____ = disproved

  3.   _____ + _____ + _____ = universal

  4. _____ + _____ + _____ + _____ = misdirected

  5.   _____ + _____ + _____ = subversive

  6.   _____ + _____ + _____ = transfusion

  7.   _____ + _____ + _____ = promotion

  8. _____ + _____ + _____ + _____ = importantly

1. _____   2. _____

3. _____   4. _____

5. _____   6. _____

7. _____   8. _____

Part 4.

1. _____   2. _____

3. _____

Part 5.

1. Always dispose of _____ in a suitable container.
   (waist, waste)

2. Do you know _____ we will be _____ to go?
   (weather, whether)   (allowed, aloud)

3. How many _____ are killed by automobiles each
   year?   (deer, dear)

waist - inside your belt	allowed - permitted	whether - if
waste - in the bin	aloud - you can hear it	weather - rain usually
dear - beloved; expensive		
deer - it has antlers		

1. _____

   _____

2. _____

   _____

3. _____

   _____

Part 6.

1.   pro + duce + ed = _____

2.   ap + prove + ed = _____

3.   sub + stant + ial = _____

4.   auto + mate + ed = _____

Part 6. Continued.

5.   in + struct + or = _____

6.   im + prove + ment = _____

7.   note + ice + ed = _____

8.   auto + mobile + s = _____

Part 7.

1. _____   2. _____

3. _____   4. _____

5. _____   6. _____

7. _____   8. _____

9. _____   10. _____

11. _____   12. _____

Part 8.

1. _____

_____

2. _____

_____

3. _____

_____

Apples and Pears

Mastery Test:

First Trial *Date:* _____

1. _____ 2. _____

3. _____ 4. _____

5. _____ 6. _____

7. _____ 8. _____

9. _____ 10. _____

11. _____ 12. _____

13. _____ 14. _____

15. _____ 16. _____

17. _____ 18. _____

19. _____ 20. _____

Second Trial *Date:* _____

1. _____ 2. _____

3. _____ 4. _____

5. _____ 6. _____

7. _____ 8. _____

9. _____ 10. _____

11. _____ 12. _____

13. _____ 14. _____

15. _____ 16. _____

17. _____ 18. _____

19. _____ 20. _____

Apples and Pears

Date: _____

Part 1.

1. _____   2. _____

3. _____   4. _____

5. _____   6. _____

Part 2.

1.   dis + ap + prove + al = _____

2.   fault + less = _____

3.   tough + ness = _____

4.   educate + ion + al = _____

5.   machine + ery = _____

6.   in + value + able = _____

7.   strange + ness = _____

8.   re + ply + ed = _____

Part 3.

      verse   prove   lieve

1. un + be + _____ + able = _____
   = a pack of lies

2. im + _____ + ing = _____
   = getting better

3. uni + _____ + ity = _____
   = where students go

Part 4.

1. _____ + _____ + _____ = _____

2. _____ + _____ + _____ = _____

3. _____ + _____ + _____ = _____

Part 5.

1. _____ 2. _____

3. _____ 4. _____

5. _____ 6. _____

Part 6.

1.   stop + ed = _____

2.   educate + ion + al = _____

3.   pro + ject + s = _____

4.   brief + ly = _____

5.   ob + ject + ive + s = _____

6.   un + be + lieve + able = _____

7.   pre + cise + ly = _____

8.   teach + er + s = _____

Part 7.

1. _____ 2. _____

3. _____ 4. _____

5. _____ 6. _____

7. _____ 8. _____

9. _____ 10. _____

11. _____ 12. _____

Apples and Pears

Part 8.

1. _____ 147

   _____

2. _____

   _____

3. _____

   _____

Part 9.

Apples and Pears

Date: _____

Part 1.

1.　　con + sume + er + s = _____

2.　　　　as + sume + ed = _____

3.　　　　re + sume + ed = _____

Part 2.

1. The shops are busy when _____ have a lot of money.

2. They _____ their voyage when the ship left port.

3. I left the door open because I _____ you were coming in.

Part 3.

1.　　　　　　　　_____ + _____ = savagely

2. _____ + _____ + _____ + _____ = unassuming

3.　　　　_____ + _____ + _____ = corrective

4.　　　　_____ + _____ + _____ = universal

5. _____ + _____ + _____ + _____ = continuation

6. _____ + _____ + _____ + _____ = compensation

7.　　　_____ + _____ + _____ = unmanageable

8.　　　　_____ + _____ + _____ = imitation

1. _____　　　2. _____

3. _____　　　4. _____

5. _____　　　6. _____

7. _____　　　8. _____

Part 4.

1. _____ 2. _____

3. _____

Part 5.

1. How many cars are parked in your sisters garage?

2. My uncles other niece is my sister.

3. Mother stopped doing my brothers laundry when he left university.

1. _____
_____

2. _____
_____

3. _____
_____

Part 6.

1.   race + ing = _____

2.   ex + act + ly = _____

3.   rot + en = _____

4.   auto + mobile = _____

5.   auto + mate + ic = _____

6.   per + miss + ion = _____

7.   un + worry + ed = _____

8.   fat + en + ing = _____

Part 7.

1. _____ 2. _____

3. _____ 4. _____

5. _____ 6. _____

7. _____ 8. _____

9. _____ 10. _____

11. _____ 12. _____

Part 8.

1. _____

_____

2. _____

_____

3. _____

_____

Apples and Pears

Date: _____

1. _____
   _____

2. _____
   _____

3. _____
   _____

4. _____
   _____

5. _____
   _____

6. _____
   _____

7. _____
   _____

8. _____
   _____

9. _____
   _____

10. _____
    _____

11. _____
    _____

12. _____
    _____

Apples and Pears

Date: _____

Part 1.

Match the following words to their meanings.

resumed •   • ate; used up

prescription •   • started again

consumed •   • a note you give to
the chemist

Part 2.

1. super + vise + ed = _____

2. en + tire = _____

3. im + prove + ment + s = _____

4. cor + rect + ing = _____

5. sale + s + man = _____

6. re + search + er = _____

7. con + sume + ing = _____

8. note + ice + able = _____

1. _____   2. _____

3. _____   4. _____

5. _____   6. _____

7. _____   8. _____

Part 3.

1. _____

_____

2. _____

_____

3. _____

_____

Apples and Pears

Part 4.

Write the words in alphabetical order.

fault

thief

autumn

laundry

chief

believe

machine

August

1. _____

2. _____

3. _____

4. _____

5. _____

6. _____

7. _____

8. _____

Part 5.

1. _____
2. _____
3. _____
4. _____
5. _____
6. _____
7. _____
8. _____
9. _____
10. _____
11. _____
12. _____
13. _____
14. _____
15. _____
16. _____
17. _____
18. _____
19. _____
20. _____
21. _____
22. _____
23. _____
24. _____

Apples and Pears

Part 6.

its - belongs to it	
it's - it is	

1. _____ essential to be on your best behavior in front of the judge.

2. A good university can rely on _____ reputation.

3. _____ a real pleasure, listening to great music on the radio.

1. _____

_____

2. _____

_____

3. _____

_____

Part 7.

Apples and Pears

Date: _____

Part 1.

1.   re + sist + ance = _____

2.   per + sist + ent + ly = _____

3.   as + sist + ing = _____

Part 2.

1. If you nag your mother _____ , you might get new trainers.

2. My sister is _____ me with my project.

3. During the war, many Frenchmen joined the

     _____ .

Part 3.

1.   _____ + _____ + _____ = relocated

2.   _____ + _____ + _____ = businesses

3.   _____ + _____ + _____ = unreliable

4.   _____ + _____ + _____ = forbidden

5.   _____ + _____ + _____ = assuming

6.   _____ + _____ + _____ = universal

7.   _____ + _____ + _____ = commotion

8.   _____ + _____ + _____ = uniformly

1. _____   2. _____

3. _____   4. _____

5. _____   6. _____

7. _____   8. _____

Apples and Pears

Part 4.

1. _____ 2. _____

3. _____

Part 5.

1. It's much easier to _____ his writing if he
   (read, reed)
   _____.
   (prints , prince)

2. Do you know _____ your dog has _____?
   (weather, whether)   (fleas, flees)

3. We got very _____ , _____ for our
   (tents, tense)   (waiting, weighting)

   teacher to return.

reed - grows on water	fleas - dogs scratch them	prints - makes letters
read - a book	flees - runs away	prince - king's son
wait - sit around	whether - if	tents - for camping
weight - how heavy it is	weather - rain usually	tense - nervous, anxious

1. _____

_____

2. _____

_____

3. _____

_____

Apples and Pears

Part 6.

1.   as + sist + ance = _____
2.   pro + test + er + s = _____
3.   list + en + ed = _____
4.   de + script + ion = _____
5.   sub + sist + ed = _____
6.   starve + ing = _____
7.   re + port = _____
8.   boil + ed = _____

Part 7.

1. _____   2. _____

3. _____   4. _____

5. _____   6. _____

7. _____   8. _____

9. _____   10. _____

11. _____   12. _____

Part 8.

1. _____

_____

2. _____

_____

3. _____

_____

Apples and Pears

Date: _____

Part 1.

1. _____ 2. _____

3. _____ 4. _____

5. _____ 6. _____

Part 2.

1. scheme + ing = _____

2. re + sist + ant = _____

3. tough + ness = _____

4. con + sume + able = _____

5. per + sist + ence = _____

6. in + con + sist + ent = _____

7. deny + ed = _____

8. character + ize + ate + ion

= _____

Part 3.

mote   ial   sist

1. con + _____ + ent = _____

= always the same

2. cord + _____ + ly = _____

= in a friendly way

3. pro + _____ + ed = _____

= given a better job or position

Part 4.

1. _____ + ___ + _____ = _____

2. ___ + _____ + _____ + ___ = _____

3. _____ + _____ + _____ = _____

Part 5.

1. _____
2. _____
3. _____
4. _____
5. _____
6. _____

Part 6.

1. cheek + y = _____
2. pre + script + ion = _____
3. be + lieve + able = _____
4. re + ceive = _____
5. anchor + ing = _____
6. race + ial = _____
7. con + fuse + ion = _____
8. machine + ery = _____

Part 7.

1. _____
2. _____
3. _____
4. _____
5. _____
6. _____
7. _____
8. _____
9. _____
10. _____
11. _____
12. _____

Part 8.

1. _____

_____

2. _____

_____

3. _____

_____

Part 9.

Arrange the words in the square so that it reads the same down and across.

mole
limp
plea
idol

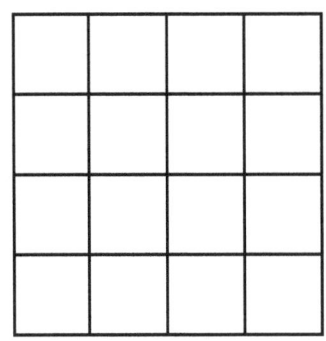

Apples and Pears

Date: _____

Part 1.

1. pre + pare + ing = _____

2. trans + pare + ent = _____

3. com + pare + ed = _____

Part 2.

1. We spent the entire weekend _____ for the test.

2. Our team hasn't done badly, _____ to last season.

3. That tissue is so thin that it is almost _____ .

Part 3.

1. _____ + _____ + _____ = departure

2. _____ + _____ = barely

3. _____ + _____ + _____ = delayed

4. _____ + _____ = writing

5. _____ + _____ + _____ = consumed

6. _____ + _____ + _____ = expelled

7. _____ + _____ + _____ = frightened

8. _____ + _____ = education

1. _____ 2. _____

3. _____ 4. _____

5. _____ 6. _____

7. _____ 8. _____

Apples and Pears

Part 4.

1. _____   2. _____

3. _____

Part 5.

1. Our ships departure was delayed by the storm.

2. Which characters do you like best?

3. I can barely read the authors writing.

1. _____

_____

2. _____

_____

3. _____

_____

Part 6.

1. auto + mobile + s = _____

2. en + count + er = _____

3. exer + cise = _____

4. pre + pare + ing = _____

5. pre + script + ion = _____

6. de + part + ment = _____

7. fault + less = _____

8. trans + port + ate + ion = _____

Apples and Pears

Part 7.

1. _____
2. _____
3. _____
4. _____
5. _____
6. _____
7. _____
8. _____
9. _____
10. _____
11. _____
12. _____

Part 8.

1. _____

_____

2. _____

_____

3. _____

_____

Apples and Pears

Date: _____

Part 1.

Match the following words to their meanings.

scheme •   • a plan

caution •   • you can see through it

transparent •   • warning; be careful

Part 2.

1.   strength + en + ed = _____

2.   as + sist + ance = _____

3.   pre + pare + ing = _____

4.   fold + ing = _____

5.   re + port + er = _____

6.   con + sist + ent + ly = _____

7.   com + pare + ing = _____

8.   chief + ly = _____

1. _____   2. _____

3. _____   4. _____

5. _____   6. _____

7. _____   8. _____

Part 3.

1. _____

_____

2. _____

_____

3. _____

_____

Apples and Pears

Part 4.

Write the words in alphabetical order.

chief   1. _____

chemist   2. _____

character   3. _____

author   4. _____

caution   5. _____

scheme   6. _____

compare   7. _____

circle   8. _____

Part 5.

1. _____   2. _____

3. _____   4. _____

5. _____   6. _____

7. _____   8. _____

9. _____   10. _____

11. _____   12. _____

13. _____   14. _____

15. _____   16. _____

17. _____   18. _____

19. _____   20. _____

21. _____   22. _____

23. _____   24. _____

Apples and Pears

Part 6.

| their - belongs to them |
| they're - they are |
| there - in that place |

1. Radio stations get many telephone calls from _____ listeners.

2. These officials spend _____ time devising all kinds of misguided schemes.

3. _____ dropping anchor in the harbour.

1. _____

   _____

2. _____

   _____

3. _____

   _____

Part 7.

Apples and Pears

Date: _____

Part 1.

1. in + clude + ing = _____

2. se + clude + ed = _____

3. con + clude + ed = _____

Part 2.

1. We found a nice _____ place to camp in the woods.

2. They finally _____ that the scheme would never work.

3. You can all come along, _____ your little brother.

Part 3.

1. _____ + _____ + _____ = transparent

2. _____ + _____ + _____ = subsisted

3. _____ + _____ + _____ = demotion

4. _____ + _____ + _____ = consumable

5. _____ + _____ + _____ + _____ = universally

6. _____ + _____ + _____ = subversive

7. _____ + _____ + _____ = amusing

8. _____ + _____ + _____ = effusive

Apples and Pears

Part 3. Continued.

1. _____   2. _____

3. _____   4. _____

5. _____   6. _____

7. _____   8. _____

Part 4.

1. _____   2. _____

3. _____

Part 5.

1. Is this package too heavy to _____ ?
   (mail , male)

2. The hunter went out and shot some old _____ .
   (dear, deer)

3. Do you _____ what size _____ _____ is?
   (no, know)   (your, you're) (waist, waste)

male - man or boy	dear - beloved; expensive	yours - belongs to you
mail - send by post	deer - it has antlers	you're - you are
no - you can't do that	waist - inside your belt	
know - understand	waste - in the bin	

1. _____

_____

2. _____

_____

3. _____

_____

Apples and Pears

Part 6.

1. con + sist + ent + ly = _____
2. se + clude + ed = _____
3. per + sist + ent = _____
4. in + clude + ing = _____
5. mis + be + have + ior = _____
6. com + pare = _____
7. per + sist + ence = _____
8. ap + prove + al = _____

Part 7.

1. _____ 2. _____
3. _____ 4. _____
5. _____ 6. _____
7. _____ 8. _____
9. _____ 10. _____
11. _____ 12. _____

Part 8.

1. _____

_____

2. _____

_____

3. _____

_____

Apples and Pears

Level 60:

Date: _____

Part 1.

1. _____   2. _____

3. _____   4. _____

5. _____   6. _____

Part 2.

1.   im + poss + ible = _____

2.   straight + en + ed = _____

3.   mount + ain + ous = _____

4.   uni + verse + ity = _____

5.   im + prove + ment = _____

6.   muse + ic = _____

7.   un + be + lieve + able = _____

8.   pro + fuse + ly = _____

Part 3.

      sist   verse   clude

1.   se + _____ + ed = _____

               = hidden away

2.   per + _____ + ent = _____

               = won't give up

3.   sub + _____ + ive = _____

               = troublemaker

Part 4.

1.   _____ + _____ + _____ = _____

2.   _____ + _____ + _____ + ____ = _____

3.   _____ + _____ + _____ = _____

Apples and Pears

Part 5.

1. _____
2. _____
3. _____
4. _____
5. _____
6. _____

Part 6.

1. sub + sist + ing = _____
2. safe + ly = _____
3. re + sponse + ible = _____
4. auto + graph = _____
5. re + fuse + al = _____
6. miss + ion = _____
7. ex + pense + ive = _____
8. post + age = _____

Part 7.

1. _____
2. _____
3. _____
4. _____
5. _____
6. _____
7. _____
8. _____
9. _____
10. _____
11. _____
12. _____

Apples and Pears

Part 8.

1. _____

   _____

2. _____

   _____

3. _____

   _____

Part 9.

Apples and Pears

Level 61:

Date: _____

Part 1.

1. col + lect = _____

2. e + lect + ion = _____

3. se + lect + ed = _____

Part 2.

1. Which party do you think will win the next _____?

2. We have _____ the choicest sausages for your enjoyment.

3. Please _____ your dirty clothes and put them in the laundry.

Part 3.

1. _____ + _____ + _____ = wealthier

2. _____ + _____ + _____ = direction

3. _____ + _____ + _____ = diversity

4. _____ + _____ + _____ + _____ = preparation

5. _____ + _____ + _____ = presuming

6. _____ + _____ + _____ = bemused

7. _____ + _____ + _____ + _____ = charcterization

8. _____ + _____ + _____ = consistent

1. _____ 2. _____

3. _____ 4. _____

5. _____ 6. _____

7. _____ 8. _____

Part 4.

1. _____   2. _____

3. _____

Part 5.

1. You should never argue with the captains decision.

2. The boys are responsible for preparing dinner tonight.

3. I have a collection of that authors books.

1. _____

_____

2. _____

_____

3. _____

_____

Part 6.

1.   situate + ion = _____

2.   se + lect + ion = _____

3.   favor + ite + s = _____

4.   re + sponse + ible = _____

5.   state + ion = _____

6.   col + lect + ion = _____

7.   straight + en + ed = _____

8.   **de** + fault = _____

Part 7.

1. _____   2. _____

3. _____   4. _____

5. _____   6. _____

7. _____   8. _____

9. _____   10. _____

11. _____   12. _____

Part 8.

1. _____

   _____

2. _____

   _____

3. _____

   _____

Apples and Pears

Date: _____

Part 1.

Match the following words to their meanings.

select •   • remember

recollect •   • finish

conclude •   • choose

Part 2.

1.   col + lect + ion = _____

2.   in + clude = _____

3.   pre + pare = _____

4.   climb + ing = _____

5.   se + lect + ed = _____

6.   im + poss + ible = _____

7.   dis + be + lieve = _____

8.   scheme + ing = _____

1. _____   2. _____

3. _____   4. _____

5. _____   6. _____

7. _____   8. _____

Part 3.

1. _____

_____

2. _____

_____

3. _____

_____

Part 4.

Write the words in alphabetical order.

select   1. _____

terrible   2. _____

straight   3. _____

compare   4. _____

chemist   5. _____

assist   6. _____

brief   7. _____

machine   8. _____

Part 5.

1. _____   2. _____

3. _____   4. _____

5. _____   6. _____

7. _____   8. _____

9. _____   10. _____

11. _____   12. _____

13. _____   14. _____

15. _____   16. _____

17. _____   18. _____

19. _____   20. _____

21. _____   22. _____

23. _____   24. _____

Apples and Pears

Part 6.

their - belongs to them there - in that place, there is, there are they're - they are	yours - belongs to you you're - you are

1. Are _____ any text messages on _____ cell phone?

2. _____ not quite sure that _____ getting a good education.

3. _____ offer to loan you an automobile might solve _____ transportation problem.

1. _____

_____

2. _____

_____

3. _____

_____

Part 7.

1. _____

_____

Part 8.

Apples and Pears

Level 63:

Date: _____

1. _____
   _____

2. _____
   _____

3. _____
   _____

4. _____
   _____

5. _____
   _____

6. _____
   _____

7. _____
   _____

8. _____
   _____

9. _____
   _____

10. _____
    _____

11. _____
    _____

12. _____
    _____